US NAVY

T0014981

BY ASHLEY STORM

Apex is distributed by North Star Editions:
sales@northstareditions.com | 888-417-0195

Produced for Apex by Red Line Editorial.

Photographs ©: Shutterstock Images, cover, 4–5, 8, 13, 16–17, 18, 19, 22–23, 29; iStockphoto, 1, 6, 14–15, 20, 24–25, 27; Wikimedia Commons, 9; U.S. Navy/Wikimedia Commons, 10–11, 12–13, 20–21; Ron Niebrugge / Alamy Stock Photo, 26

Library of Congress Control Number: 2022901406

ISBN
978-1-63738-315-5 (hardcover)
978-1-63738-351-3 (paperback)
970-1-63738 410 0 (ebook pdf)
978-1-63738-387-2 (hosted ebook)

Printed in the United States of America
Mankato, MN
082022

TABLE OF CONTENTS

CHAPTER 1

SNEAK ATTACK

The sea is calm. Deep underwater, a US Navy **submarine** moves quickly and silently. It can sink ships. It can blow airplanes out of the sky. No one knows it is there.

Submarines can travel above or below the water.

The sailors on the submarine are on a secret mission. They are tracking an enemy ship. They prepare to shoot it.

FAST FACT

The US Navy has more than 70 submarines.

A tool called a periscope allows people in a submarine to see things above the water.

Some torpedoes can travel up to 50 miles per hour (80 km/h).

The submarine fires a torpedo. It hits the target. The enemy's ship sinks. The mission is a success.

THE FIRST FIGHT

A submarine was first used in battle in 1776. It was called the *Turtle*. It could only fit one person. Today, US Navy submarines can hold more than 100 sailors.

The *Turtle* was only about 7.5 feet (2.3 m) long and 6 feet (1.8 m) wide.

CHAPTER 2

NAVY HISTORY

An early version of the US Navy began in 1775. It was called the Continental Navy. It helped American **colonies** fight in the Revolutionary War (1775–1783).

The Continental Navy had about 60 ships.

After the war, the Continental Navy **disbanded**. But the United States needed protection. So, it founded the US Navy in 1798.

PIRATES!

In the late 1700s, pirates attacked US ships. They stole the ships' cargo. They held people for ransom. The government sent US Navy ships to fight back.

The US Navy continues to protect ships from pirates.

The US Navy has protected the United States for hundreds of years. It fought against Japan during World War II (1939–1945).

Over the years, the Navy grew. It built more ships. And it began using aircraft. The Navy has used them to fight in many wars.

F-35C jets fly very fast and high. They are hard for enemies to spot.

The F-35C is the US Navy's fastest jet. It can fly more than 1,200 miles per hour (1,931 km/h).

CHAPTER 3

BECOMING A SAILOR

To join the Navy, people must go to boot camp. This training prepares people for life at sea. They learn how work as a team. They learn how to live in small spaces.

Training for the US Navy lasts 10 weeks.

Some Navy sailors guide planes. They help the planes take off and land on ships.

After boot camp, sailors train for certain jobs. Some learn to fix things. Others become divers. The Navy has doctors and scientists, too.

US NAVY BAND

The US Navy has a band. Band members go through boot camp, just like other sailors. Then they practice and play at special events.

Members of the US Navy band play many types of instruments.

Some sailors become officers. They lead groups of people. A captain runs one ship. An admiral leads many ships.

Officers wear bars or pins on their uniforms to show their ranks.

Aircraft carriers are large ships. Many sailors work together to run them.

CHAPTER 4

LIFE IN THE NAVY

Navy sailors do many types of missions around the world. They work on ships or submarines. They stay at sea for months.

The US Navy often uses small, fast ships called destroyers. These ships carry weapons.

The Navy has many types of ships and submarines. Some ships are built for fighting. Others carry airplanes. All help keep Americans safe.

FAST FACT

The largest Navy ships have more than 5,000 people aboard. They are like small cities.

Some US Navy aircraft carriers can hold up to 90 airplanes.

There is a large naval base in San Diego, California.

After a mission, most sailors go back to a Navy **base**. Each base has many homes and buildings. Sailors may live there with their families. Some officers work there, too.

SPECIAL FORCES

The US Navy has special forces teams. These groups carry out difficult missions. Some spy on enemies. Some fight terrorists. Others rescue people.

Members of the Navy's special forces work in small teams. They often do secret missions.

COMPREHENSION QUESTIONS

Write your answers on a separate piece of paper.

1. Write a few sentences that explain the main ideas of Chapter 2.

2. Which type of job in the US Navy would you be most interested in having? Why?

3. When was the US Navy founded?

    A. 1776

    B. 1798

    C. 1945

4. Why would submarines be useful for secret missions?

    A. Submarines are really heavy.

    B. Submarines can move without being seen.

    C. Submarines do not carry any weapons.

5. What does **mission** mean in this book?

The sailors on the submarine are on a secret mission. They are tracking an enemy ship.

    A. important job or goal

    B. vacation

    C. field trip

6. What does **target** mean in this book?

The submarine fires a torpedo. It hits the target. The enemy's ship sinks.

    A. something people cannot see

    B. something people try to shoot

    C. something high in the air

Answer key on page 32.

GLOSSARY

base
An area where navy ships are kept when not in use.

cargo
Items carried by a ship from one place to another.

colonies
Areas that are ruled by a different country.

disbanded
Broke up.

ransom
Money paid to get back something that was taken.

special forces
Groups of the military who get extra training and do work such as spying or surprise attacks.

submarine
A ship that can stay deep underwater for a long time.

terrorists
People who attack and scare others to reach their goals.

torpedo
An underwater missile.

TO LEARN MORE

BOOKS

Brody, Walt. *How Submarines Work*. Minneapolis: Lerner Publishing, 2019.

Hustad, Douglas. *US Navy Equipment and Vehicles*. Minneapolis: Abdo Publishing, 2021.

Morey, Allan. *U.S. Navy*. Minneapolis: Jump!, 2021.

ONLINE RESOURCES

Visit **www.apexeditions.com** to find links and resources related to this title.

ABOUT THE AUTHOR

Ashley Storm has written more than 20 books for children and teens. She lives in Kentucky with her husband, three mischievous cats, and a flock of bossy backyard chickens who peck on the door to demand treats. Her father is a US Navy veteran.

INDEX

ANSWER KEY:
1. Answers will vary; 2. Answers will vary; 3. B; 4. B; 5. A; 6. B